To Sarah - Dorothy...

Nancy Carlson 1984

Bunnies and Their Hobbies

Bunnies and Their Hobbies

A fter a long day at work,

by Nancy Carlson

Carolrhoda Books, Inc., Minneapolis

bunnies come home,

Library of Congress Cataloging in Publication Data

Carlson, Nancy, L.
  Bunnies and their hobbies.

  Summary: Describes the many activities bunnies like to
spend time on after "a long day at work."
  [1. Rabbits—Fiction. 2. Hobbies—Fiction] I. Title
PZ7.C21665Bu 1984 [E] 83-23161
ISBN 0-87614-257-9 (lib. bdg.)

1 2 3 4 5 6 7 8 9 10 90 89 88 87 86 85 84

change their clothes,

*To Uncle Bill and his hobbies, Aunt Char, and
all our great times at the lake*

eat dinner,

and do the dishes.
Then it's time for
bunnies and their hobbies.

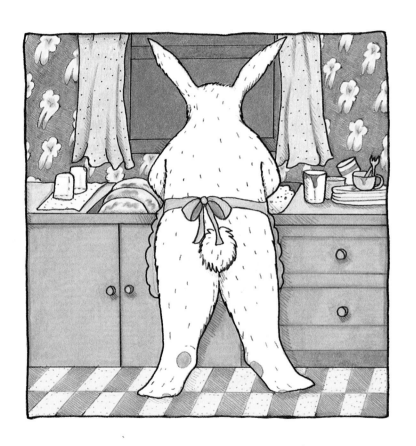

Some bunnies like to do a little yardwork
in the evenings.

Others would rather sunbathe.

Bunnies who appreciate dance
may go to an aerobic dance class
or learn the latest steps
at Arthur Murray.

Bowling is a favorite hobby of many bunnies.
So is playing cards.

Artistic bunnies paint pictures
or go to museums.
Musical bunnies play instruments.

Concerned bunnies often volunteer
to help others.

Many bunnies are collectors.
Some collect stamps.
Others collect aluminum cans.

Handy bunnies build things,
like birdhouses.

Romantic bunnies like to fall in love.

It's not uncommon to find outdoor bunnies
fishing or playing soccer.

Quiet bunnies prefer to read a book
or doze in a favorite chair.

Different bunnies enjoy different hobbies,
but when bedtime comes,
all bunnies like to go to sleep.

Sweet dreams, bunnies.